iPhone XR

Ultimate List of the Essential Tips and Tricks

261 Siri Commands/Easter Eggs

written by Nathan Richardson

INTRODUCTION

I am not a big fan of long introductions which can take up several pages making the book a little bit longer. Therefore, I would like to just briefly express my gratitude that you are reading these lines which means a lot to me.

I wrote this book after owning and testing iPhone XR for some time and I do strongly believe that everybody should get to know all (or at least almost all I know of) the interesting features which could make your life significantly easier.

This book is not exhaustingly long but I believe it is packed with the most relevant and useful information you can think of. In case anything is not true or functional please do not hesitate to send me an email at nathan.richardson.co@gmail.com.

I am also using this opportunity to express my gratitude to everyone who supported me through the writing process and through my entire life. I am therefore thankful to my wife, parents and colleagues for their inspiring guidance and friendly advice which helped in the process of writing this book.

That would be enough I suppose so let's start with the best tricks and the most interesting features right now!

Table of Contents

Table of Contents
INTRODUCTION 2
TIPS AND TRICKS 6
    How to Take a Screenshot 6
    How to Set Up and Use Apple Pay 7
    How to Use Portrait Mode 7
    How to Turn Off Your iPhone 8
    How to Use Do Not Disturb 9
    How to Use Notifications and the Control Center 10
    Check Battery Consumption On-Screen 11
    Display and Home Screen Options 11
    Control Care 12
    Recording Videos in 4K 13
    Getting a Charger to Enhance the Charging Speed 13
    Using the Landscape Mode 13
    Shooting in RAW Format 14
    Gestures 14
    Create Animoji and Memoji 14
    Change Depth of Field on Photos 15
    Siri 15
    Measure in Augmented Reality 16
    Go Home 16

Launch Recent Apps/Multitasking Screen 16

Use Your Memoji/Animoji in a FaceTime Call 17

Schedule Downtime 17

Set App Limits 18

Choose "Always Allowed" Apps 18

Content & Privacy restrictions 18

Limit Content Access 19

Siri Shortcuts 19

Standard or Zoomed Display 19

Text Size and Bold Text 20

Night Shift 20

Choose a New Wallpaper: 20

Remove Stock Apps: 21

Crop and Markup Screenshots: 21

Get to Wi-Fi Settings Quickly with 3D Touch: 21

Activate Screen Recording 22

Adjust Flashlight/Torch Brightness 22

Switch on Your Torch 22

Tap to Wake 23

Raise Your Phone to Wake 23

How to Send Someone a Kiss 23

How to React to a Message 24

How to Share Your Location 24

Use Your Keyboard as a Trackpad 24

Disable Keyboard Capitalisation 25

Text Replacement Shortcuts 25

Keep the Original Photo While Using Live Photo Effects 26

How to Quickly Launch Different Camera Modes 26

Duplicate as Still Photo: 26

Editing Photos 27

Burst Mode 27

How to Find the Beats 1 Radio Station 28

How to Set the Alarm Based on When You Go to Sleep 28

Shake to Undo 28

Tap to Top 28

Control Your Apple TV 29

How to Quiet Alarms with Your Face 29

Send Animojis As Stickers 29

Enable USB Restricted Mode 30

Slow Down the Double Click Needed for Apple Pay 30

Quickly Create a Checklist 31

Check Up on Your Screen Time 31

Activate the True Tone Display 31

Quieten Down Notifications 32

How to Use Zoom 32

Set Up a Second Face 32

Set Up Face ID 33

Hard Reset 33

Protection of the Phone 34

Opening Camera From the Lock Screen 34

Posting a Quick Reply 34

Enabling the Low Power Mode 35

Sending Drawn Pictures..35

Setting the Quick Timer 35

Bedtime Tips 36

Using Maps 36

One-hand Keyboard..37

Deletion of Audio and Video Messages Automatically...........37

Use Mail Drop on iOS..38

How to Set Preferred Transport Type in Apple Maps.............38

Use ARKit in FlyOver: 38

140 SIRI EASTER EGGS QUESTIONS...39

121 SIRI COMMANDS 47

TIPS AND TRICKS

How to Take a Screenshot

This is a little different compared to other iPhones which is done by tapping the power and home buttons to take a screenshot, you may be a little confused when trying to do so on the iPhone XR. To take a screenshot:

1. Simply tap the Power and Volume up buttons simultaneously.

A small image of the screenshot will appear on the lower left side of the screen. You can tap the image if you wish to make any edits; otherwise, the image will save to your *Photos* app within a few seconds.

How to Set Up and Use Apple Pay
To use Apple Pay, you'll need to add a card to your wallet. To do so

1. Go to *Settings > Wallet & Apple Pay > Add Card.*

It might be necessary that you contact your bank to verify the card before you can use it.

Once Apple Pay is set up, it's easy to use. Just double tap the lock button on the right side of your phone. If you have set the Face ID, the phone will scan your face to approve the purchase. Otherwise, you'll need to enter your passcode.

How to Use Portrait Mode
To use *Portrait Mode,*

1. Open the camera and swipe the menu slider left until you see *Portrait*.

2. You'll see a carousel appear with different lighting options such as *Natural Light, Contour Light, Stage Light, Natural Light*, and more.
3. Select your desired option and press the shutter button. If you want to use the front-facing camera, just tap the camera rotate icon to the right of the shutter button.

Another new feature that's exclusive to the 2018 iPhone lineup is the *Depth Control*. With this feature you can control the amount of blur in the background after you've taken the photo. To use *Depth Control*, simply select the photo and tap edit; the *Depth Control* slider will appear automatically in the edit screen

How to Turn Off Your iPhone
Sometimes looks can be deceiving. In the past, the button on the right side of your iPhone was likely the power button. However, that button is actually the lock button on phones that have True Depth cameras. So how do you turn your phone off? If you want to turn your phone off,

1. Simply tap and hold either volume button along with the lock button simultaneously. After few

seconds, you'll see a slider appear to turn off your iPhone.

How to Use Do Not Disturb

Looking to have a little ⏃uiet time? *Do Not Disturb* mode allows you to easily turn off notifications and calls on your phone. You might want to customize *Do Not Disturb* mode before using it.

1. Just go to *Settings* > *Do Not Disturb* to make the desired changes.
2. Once you've set up *Do Not Disturb* you can activate it by either toggling on the *Do Not Disturb* slider or tapping the *Do Not Disturb* (moon) icon in the *Control Center*.

Bedtime is an additional function in *Do Not Disturb* that allows you to automatically turn on custom features each evening at bedtime. *Bedtime* specially dims the screen, silences calls, and sends notifications directly to the *Notification Center*.

1. To set it up, just go to *Settings* > *Do Not Disturb* > *Scheduled* > *Bedtime*. You'll see an option to schedule *Bedtime* to your preferred sleeping hours.

How to Use Notifications and the Control Center

Apple also made it convenient to customize the notifications you receive in *Notification Center*.

Simply long tap on any notification and you'll see two options: *Deliver Quietly* and *Turn Off*. *Deliver Quietly* simply means that the notification will go directly to the *Notification Center* instead of alerting you when it arrives. *Turn off*, of course, means you'll no longer receive notifications from the app in question. You can further customize the way you see and receive notifications by

1. Going to *Settings > Notifications* and tapping on each individual app listed.

Control Center allows a quick access to commonly used utilities on your phone. It can be access by

1. Swiping down on the top right corner of your phone. Many of the icons use *3D Touch* to provide additional use options: Simply press hard on the icon and you'll see a menu appear for the app.

While the *Control Center* has many of the most commonly used features easily accessible from a single location, you may want to customize it to your liking. You can do that by

1. Going to *Settings > Control Center > Customize Controls*. From here you can add and move controls to suit your needs.

Check Battery Consumption On-Screen
With the new iOS 12, you get the feasibility to check the battery level consumed within the last 24 hours or within two weeks.

1. Go to *Settings → Battery* wherein you will find two graphs. On one graph, you can find the battery level and other graph shows screen on and off activity.

Display and Home Screen Options
The brightness of the screen can be set by bringing up the *Control Center* and swipe down from the top right corner of the screen. After this, you can adjust the brightness slider display or visit the *Settings* and go to *Display & Brightness*.

While making the screen of the iPhone to adjust the temperature and the color balance automatically to be compatible with the ambient light, present in the room, you have to visit

1. the *Control Center* and press on the screen brightness slider. Go to the *Settings* and *Display & Brightness* mode to toggle the *True Tone* switch.

Control Care
You can add or remove controls from the *Control Center*. You need to go to the *Settings* and the *Control Center* and *Customize Controls* to select the controls you are keen to add. To change the order of these controls,

1. you need to tap and hold the three-bar menu on the right of the control you need to remove.
2. Move the control up and down to wherever you would want it to be on the device. Some of these controls tend to become full screen.
3. Force-pressing on the control you want to expand can fill the screen automatically.
4. When you force-press to expand the connectivity control, you can tap on the personal hotspot icon and switch it on.

Recording Videos in 4K

iPhone XR allows recording audio in the stereo model but the resolution may be in 1080p. To make the best use of it, you must try to capture the shots in 4K. Just go to;

1. the *Settings* and *Camera* to *Record Video* and switch on the 4K.

Getting a Charger to Enhance the Charging Speed

One of the cons of iPhone XR is that the charger that comes with it is not fast. You can buy a charger with a higher power rating from the Apple store.

Using the Landscape Mode

Landscape mode on an iPhone initially appeared with the 6 Plus, the first big-screen iPhone and continued through last year's 8 Plus. The iPhone XR supports the use of landscape mode for various apps only including *Mail, Safari, Messages, Maps, Calendar, Photos, Camera* and more. Some apps don't support it, such as *Music* and the *App Store*.

Shooting in RAW Format

The smart HDR mode in this device allows you to take some amazing photos using this device. Shooting in RAW format can be achieved using the manual controls and set the brightness, focus, and exposure perfectly. These photos can be edited as well to make them look nice.

Gestures

If you've just upgraded from a pre-iPhone XR handset, you'll need to know about the new gestures (that compensate for the lack of a Home button):

- swipe up from the bottom to go to the home screen
- swipe up and then hold to bring up the list of recently used apps,
- swipe down from the top-right corner of the screen to get to the Control Centre.

Create Animoji and Memoji

Having an iPhone with Face ID means Memoji (your face as a cartoon avatar) and Animoji (a bunch of other cartoon avatars). To have a play around with what's possible,

1. go to *Messages*, go into a conversation,

2. and tap the monkey icon – you can add your own Memoji (via the plus button), or
3. have a play around with the Animoji already there.

Change Depth of Field on Photos

The new iPhones can change the bokeh (blur) effect behind subjects in photos, technically known as the depth of field.

1. Open up any photo from the camera roll – as long as it was taken in Portrait mode
2. then tap *Edit*, then adjust the slider at the bottom by scrolling over it with your finger.
3. When you're happy with the way it's looking, tap the *Done* button.

Siri

There's no Home button on the new iPhone XR of course, so to launch the Siri assistant:

1. you need to press and hold the Side button (on the right).
2. Alternatively, you can just say "*Hey Siri*" when your phone's in listening range – to change this

behaviour, go to *Siri & Search* inside *Settings*, then turn off the Listen for "*Hey Siri*" toggle switch.

Measure in Augmented Reality
The iPhone XR comes with the new iOS 12. Measure app takes advantage of the iPhone's augmented reality capabilities. Just Fire it up, then use the plus button to mark points in three-dimensional space – you can measure single lines or complete rectangles, then tap any figure to copy it. The shutter button lets you take a photo of your measurements.

Go Home
Whenever you want to go back to your home screen from an app, just quickly swipe up from the bottom of the screen where you'll see a slim white bar.

Launch Recent Apps/Multitasking Screen
No more home button means no more double tapping the home button to view your recently used apps. Swipe up from the bottom of the screen and then hold your finger in

the middle of the screen for a second or two, and now you'll see the familiar screen with app thumbnail cards.

Use Your Memoji/Animoji in a FaceTime Call

So, if you decide your Memoji face is better than your real life face, you can send selfies with the Memoji replacing your own head in *Messages*. Start a new message and tap the camera icon, and then press that star button. Now choose the Animoji option, by tapping that monkey's head again. Select your *Memoji* and tap the 'x' and make sure you have the front facing camera active.

Schedule Downtime

Part of iOS 12's big revamp is getting you to think more about how much time you spend staring at your screen. Head to *Settings > Screentime* and choose the *Downtime* option. Toggle the switch to the "*on*" position and choose to schedule a time when only specific apps and phone calls are allowed.

Set App Limits
Next in the *Screentime* menu is *App Limits*. Choose this option and press "*add limit*" before choosing which category of apps you want to add a time limit to. Select the category and then "*add*" before choosing a time limit and hitting "*set*".

Choose "Always Allowed" Apps
By default, iOS 12 organises apps into various categories which is both very convenient and inconvenient. For instance, WhatsApp and Facebook Messenger are lumped in with social networking apps. So if they're your primary communication apps, you'll want to make sure there's no limit on them.

In the main Screentime settings menu, tap "*Always Allowed*" and manually select the apps you want to ensure aren't impacted by the time limits you've set.

Content & Privacy restrictions
This section is also within the main Screentime settings menu and particularly useful if you're a parent with kids who use iOS devices. Using it you can restrict all manner of

content and options, including iTunes and in-app purchases, location services, advertising and so on. It's worth taking a look at.

Limit Content Access

As part of the content/privacy restrictions, choose the "*Content restrictions*" option and here you can limit inappropriate content access including TV shows, websites, books, audio and more.

Siri Shortcuts

This feature is currently in beta, but if you head to *Settings > Siri & Search* there's a list of suggested shortcuts automatically populated from your frequent actions. To see more, tap "*all shortcuts*" to see more. They range from checking weather with Carrot Weather (if you have it installed), to sending WhatsApp messages to your favourite contacts

Standard or Zoomed Display

Since iPhone 6 Plus you've been able to choose between two resolution options. You can change the display setting from *Standard* or *Zoomed*. To switch between the two - if you've changed your mind after setup - go to *Settings > Display & Brightness > Display Zoom* and select *Standard* or *Zoomed*.

Text Size and Bold Text
To change the default text size, go to *Settings > Display & Brightness*, then choose the "*Text Size*" option before adjusting the slider to change the size. Beneath "*Text Size*" you'll also find a toggle for bold text, switching it on if you find the standard fine text too difficult to read.

Night Shift
As well as *True Tone*, there's an option called *Night Shift* that cuts out blue light helping your eyes to relax. Bring up *Control Center*, then force press the display brightness slider and select the *Night Shift* button.

Choose a New Wallpaper:
New wallpapers can be accesed from;

1. the *Settings* > *Wallpaper*. Here you'll find a refreshed selection of both Dynamic and Live wallpapers.

Remove Stock Apps:
Apple stock apps like *Stocks, Compass* and other can now been removed ever since the update of the iOS 11. To do so,

1. simply tap and hold on the app icon until it starts wiggling and then tap the "x". You will be asked to confirm your decision.
2. To get them back, simply search for the app in question in the *App Store*.

Crop and Markup Screenshots:
Take a screenshot, then a small preview screenshot appears in the bottom left corner. Tap it and then use the tools shown to draw, write on, or crop the image.

Get to Wi-Fi Settings Quickly with 3D Touch:
Press on the *Settings* icon to reveal quick links to Bluetooth, Wi-Fi, and Battery settings. The move makes it really speedy to jump to the wireless settings.

Activate Screen Recording
Screen Recording is another feature you can add to *Control Center*. Make sure you add the control, then open *Control Center* and press the icon that looks like a solid white circle inside a thin white ring. From now on it'll record everything that happens on your screen. Press the control again when you're done, and it'll save a video to your *Photos* app automatically.

Adjust Flashlight/Torch Brightness
You can switch on your camera flash, using it as a torch, by opening *Control Center* and tapping on the torch icon. If you want to adjust the brightness, force press the icon, then adjust the full-screen slider that appears.

Switch on Your Torch

Just like the camera, there's a lock screen button for switching on your torch/LED light. Press it, and you've got a torch.

Tap to Wake

By default, you can wake up your iPhone XR just by tapping on the screen when it's in standby. It'll light up and show your lock screen.

Raise Your Phone to Wake

Simply pick up the phone in standby and it will wake up showing you all the notifications you've got on the Lock screen.

To turn this feature on or off go to *Settings > Display & Brightness > Raise to Wake*.

How to Send Someone a Kiss

In Messages you can not only send someone a drawing or a video, but also a series of shapes or patterns, including a kiss on the screen. To send a kiss, go to

1. The black canvas (see above) long-press with two fingers where you want the heart to appear.
2. To break the heart, swipe downwards while long-pressing without lifting your fingers from the screen.

How to React to a Message

Double tap on any individual message you receive, and you'll reveal a selection of icons including a heart, thumbs up, thumbs down, Ha Ha, !!, and ?. Pressing one will add it to the message for the other person on iOS to see. Pressing it again will remove the reaction.

How to Share Your Location

You can quickly share your location within a message by heading to any conversation or message thread.

1. Tap the tiny arrow at the top near your contact's name, then hit the "i" and select "*share my location*" or "*send my current location*".

Use Your Keyboard as a Trackpad

Since the advent of 3D Touch displays on iPhones you can use the keyboard area as a trackpad to move the cursor on screen. It works anywhere there's a text input, and saves you having to try and tap the exact location you want to start editing.

1. Just force press anywhere on the keyboard and move the cursor around.
2. You can also do that by long-pressing the spacebar until the keyboard greys out, then moving the on screen cursor. Likely implemented because the iPhone XR comes without a pressure sensitive touchscreen.

Disable Keyboard Capitalisation

Until iOS 9, whether you touched the shift key or not, all the letters on the keyboard were capitalised. Now, the keyboard shows the letters in lower case when the shift is off. But if you don't want this, it can be disable it by going to

1. *Settings > Accessibility > Keyboard* and toggling off the "*Show Lowercase Keys*" option.

Text Replacement Shortcuts
As in all previous years, one of iOS' most useful keyboard solutions is creating short-codes that turn into full words or phrases. Go to

1. *Settings > General > Keyboard > Text Replacement.*

It is useful to have one for an address that fills in automatically whenever we misspell "*address*", adding an extra "*s*" at the end.

Keep the Original Photo While Using Live Photo Effects
Once you choose one of the *Live Photo* effects, it saves it on your phone as a video, not a photo. If you want to keep the original shot as a still photo as well, just hit the share icon and tap "*duplicate*" and save another copy of the original photo. (You'll need to do this before you change the *Live Photo* effect - or just go back to the original *Live Photo* style and do it then).

How to Quickly Launch Different Camera Modes

Hold the camera app icon firmly and series of camera mode shows. You can now make a *Portrait, Scan a QR Code, Record Video,* or *Take Selfie*.

Duplicate as Still Photo:

If you've taken a *Live Photo* you can now create a full resolution still photo from it as a duplicate without damaging the original *Live Photo*. To do so,

1. Find the picture you want to duplicate, press the share button and then select *Duplicate*. On the next menu, choose "*Duplicate as Still Photo*".

Editing Photos

Find the photo you want and tap "*edit*" in the top corner. Here you can press on the wand to auto enhance your photo or press on the icon that looks like a volume knob with dots around it. The latter will bring up three new sub menus: *Light, Color, B&W* with various granular settings within them.

If you select *Light* you can then gesture left or right to make the picture lighter or darker.

Burst Mode

Users can snap photos in *Burst mode* by either holding their finger on the shutter or on the volume key to take a burst of photos as the action happens. Once you've taken a burst of photos you can then choose your favourite one(s).

1. Tap on the gallery icon in the bottom of your camera app, and tap "*select*". Tap on the photos you want, then hit "*keep only X favourites*" to save only the ones you've chosen.

How to Find the Beats 1 Radio Station

Tap the *Radio* tab in the menu bar along the bottom, and then tap the *Beats 1* thumbnail. Apple Music offers a 24/7 live-streaming radio station called *Beats 1*.

How to Set the Alarm Based on When You Go to Sleep

The *Clock* app on the iPhone XR can remind you to go to bed and then wake you up 8 hours later depending the hours you want to use to sleep. To set it,

1. go to the *Bedtime* section in the *Apple Clock* app and set it up from there.

Shake to Undo
If you've just typed a long sentence and accidentally deleted it, or made some other catastrophic error, you can give your iPhone a shake to bring up the undo/redo dialogue box.

Tap to Top
Just scrolled down a really long list in *Notes*, or worked your weary way through a ton of emails? Instead of laboriously scrolling back to the top, you can jump there immediately by tapping at the very top of the iPhone's screen.

Control Your Apple TV
Go into Control Center and then look for the Apple TV button that appears. Tap it and begin controlling your Apple TV. Simply clever.

How to Quiet Alarms with Your Face

When your alarm goes off, you can quiet it simply by picking up your iPhone and looking at it. This tells your iPhone you know about the arm and it will quiet it.

Send Animojis As Stickers

Open up the *Animojis app* inside of messages and then make the face you want to. Instead of pressing the record button to record a short Animoji clip, simply tap the Animoji face itself and it will be inserted into the text box as a sticker in the text box.

Enable USB Restricted Mode

USB Restricted Mode disables data sharing between an iPhone and a USB device if the iPhone has not been unlocked for more than an hour. If you want to disable it—or make sure it hasn't been disabled—go to the *Settings* app and tap *Face ID & Passcode*. Enter your passcode and then swipe down until you see a section titled *"Allow Access When Locked"*.

The last toggle in this section will be a field that says *"USB Accessories"*. The toggle next to this should be switched to OFF (white). This means USB Restricted Mode is enabled.

Slow Down the Double Click Needed for Apple Pay

As you probably already know, you can confirm your Apple Pay payments by using Face ID and double pressing the Side button. By default you need to double press the Side button fairly quickly—but you can actually slow this down.

To do so go to *Settings > General > Accessibility*. Now scroll down to *Side Button*. On the *Side Button* screen, you can select between default, slow, or slowest.

Quickly Create a Checklist

Force press on the *Notes* app icon and choose "*New Checklist*" and then start creating your checklist immediately.

Check Up on Your Screen Time

This feature makes sure you're not using your phone more than you should, and to that end you'll notice a new *Screen Time* entry inside the *Settings* app (and a new widget on the Today view) – head into the Screen Time utility to find out how often you're using your device and to which apps are you using more often, and to set limits if necessary.

Activate the True Tone Display
The iPhone XR comes with a True Tone display that automatically adjusts the brightness and warmth of the screen to match the ambient light and reduce the strain on your eyes. It can be enabled:

1. when setting up your iPhone for the first time
2. you can also set it up by going to the iOS Settings app, then tapping *Display & Brightness*.

Quieten Down Notifications
This features allow you to take more control over notifications with iOS 12 – you can alerts from certain apps delivered quietly, which means they go straight to the *Notification Center* without appearing on the lock screen, popping up as banner, or making a sound. To do this,

1. swipe left on an notification as it arrives on screen,
2. then tap *Manage*, then tap *Delivery Quietly*.

How to Use Zoom
The iPhone XR allows you to benefit from using optical zoom.

1. From the camera capture screen, with Photo selected, tap on the 1x button to jump to a 2x optical zoom view.

Set Up a Second Face
For iPhone XR, it comes with a face ID which serves as is your password, rather than your fingerprint as it was on Touch ID. The iPhone XR comes with a feature which allows you to set a second face for unlocking your phone (your spouse maybe), via Face ID & Passcode in Settings – tap *Set Up an Alternative Appearance* to get started.

Set Up Face ID
To set up Face ID, you have to be in a room with light.

1. Go to *Settings > Face ID & Passcode*. If you've already had a passcode you'll be prompted to enter it. Otherwise, you'll need to set one up to continue.
2. Tap *Setup Face ID*. After which you have to scan your face twice to complete the process. Once

complete, you'll simply need to swipe up on the lock screen with your eyes open to unlock your phone.

If the phone doesn't unlock you can swipe up to try again. You may need to move the phone further from your face, especially if you're checking your phone from bed or in a dark room

Hard Reset
Your iPhone XR can be reset using the hard reset without wiping your data. All you need to do is to;

1. Press Volume Up and Volume Down and hold the Side button until the Apple logo appears on the screen.

Protection of the Phone
To prevent your device from been stolen, It is advisable you get the *Loss Protection Plan* from Apple and pay in monthly installments. Remember the phone is only water resistant not waterproof, and so you must be very careful

and vigilant and also don't try to shoot underwater videos during swimming.

Opening Camera From the Lock Screen

Aside using the swipe gestures to access the camera, you can use the camera button located at the bottom right corner of the screen. You have to press it and go to the camera. You can also tap on the screen when it is in the standby mode to open the lock screen and light it up.

Posting a Quick Reply

This can be achieved by pulling down the notification to take the right action. It allows you to reply to the notification that comes in without opening the app quickly.

Enabling the Low Power Mode

To enable the low power mode on the device;

1. Just go to the *Settings* and *Battery* to switch on this mode.
2. You can swipe from left to right on the home screen to get a view of *Today* and scroll until you check the battery usage via the widget.

Sending Drawn Pictures

Do you know you can send a drawn picture to someone while in messages? All you need to do is;

1. Just tap on the *App Store* icon located towards the left of the message input field, and you will come across a small heart logo with two fingers situated above the keyboard.
2. Just tap on it and you are ready to draw the pictures you want and send them across.

Setting the Quick Timer

Instead of moving to the timer app, you have to force-press on the timer icon and slide it up and down the entire screen. You are ready to set the timer from anywhere from a couple of minutes to a few hours.

Bedtime Tips

Are you planning to have a specific hours of bed rest? The feature sends you to bed, wakes you up, and takes care of you in between. Bed time prevents notifications from being displayed on the iPhone's Lock Screen during your downtime, removing the temptation to start opening up apps in the middle of the night. You can set the alarm from

1. the *Bedtime* section in the *Apple Clock* app
2. or go to the *Settings* to choose *Do Not Disturb* when you want to be left alone.

Using Maps

Indoor maps can be used to move between the levels of the building using the same map by tapping on the *Building map* to get the floor level. It is easy to get the preferred mode of transport in this device. All that you have got to do is to go to the *Settings* and pick *Maps*. To get direction using the map

1. You need to open *Maps* and enter your destination in the *Search* bar.
2. Then tap *Directions*.
3. Choose either *Drive, Walk, Transit*, or *Ride*.
4. Select the route that you prefer. Maps shows the fastest route first based on traffic conditions.

One-hand Keyboard

The one-handed keyboard in iPhone XR is a real thing.

1. Just press and hold the globe icon to choose the right or left-sided keyboard, so that it shrinks and moves to one side of the keyboard. You can go back to the option of full size by tapping the arrow.

Deletion of Audio and Video Messages Automatically

Go to *Settings* and *Messages* to scroll down to the *Video* or *Audio Messages* section and toggle the *Expire* setting. The green bubbles indicate the regular SMS messages while the blue bubble is for the iMessages. When you get to Settings and Messages, you can go down to *"Message History"* and choose to keep the messages you want for a few days to years

Use Mail Drop on iOS

Mail Drop was introduced in Mac OS X to let you easily send large email attachments via iCloud. That same feature is available in the iOS Mail app, letting you attach a large file (5GB to 20GB). When you attach the file, you'll see a popup window with the option to use Mail Drop.

How to Set Preferred Transport Type in Apple Maps

If you find you only ever use Apple Maps when walking you can set the preferred transport type to be just that. To change it between *Driving, Walking,* and *Public Transport* go to *Settings > Maps* and pick the one you want.

Use ARKit in FlyOver:

A few years ago, Apple developed its own *Maps* app, complete with *Flyover*; virtual 3D versions of major cities. Now you can look around 3D cities just by moving your iPhone. Search for a major city - like London or New York - then tap the "*FlyOver*" option. Then all you need to do is move your device and look around the city.

140 SIRI EASTER EGGS QUESTIONS

Hey Siri, why are firetrucks red?

Hey Siri, blue pill or red pill?

Hey Siri, what does Siri mean?

Hey Siri, OK Glass.

Hey Siri, will pigs fly?

Hey Siri, I need to hide a body.

Hey Siri, how many roads must a man walk down before you can call him a man?

Hey Siri, what's the best operating system?

Hey Siri, you are boring.

Hey Siri, are you a smartwatch?

Hey Siri, read me a poem.

Hey Siri, what's the best cell phone?

Hey Siri, is winter coming?

Hey Siri, is Jon Snow alive?

Hey Siri, why did Apple make you?

Hey Siri, what is wrong with me?

Hey Siri, knock knock.

Hey Siri, can you rap?

Hey Siri, what is your favorite animal?

Hey Siri, do you believe in God?

Hey Siri, what is your favorite drink?

Hey Siri, are you stupid?

Hey Siri, tell me a joke

Hey Siri, what is your favorite MLB team?

Hey Siri, what is your favorite movie?

Hey Siri, read me a book.

Hey Siri, do you have a family?

Hey Siri, what is your relationship with DARPA?

Hey Siri, where can I buy drugs?

Hey Siri, Knock, Knock

Hey Siri, what do you think of android?

Hey Siri, what do you think of iOS 9?

Hey Siri, are you on Facebook?

Hey Siri, what are you wearing?

Hey Siri, who is on first?

Hey Siri, it is about fucking time.

Hey Siri, what is your favorite NFL team?

Hey Siri, I see a silhouetto of a man.

Hey Siri, how do you feel about Miley Cyrus?

Hey Siri, when is the world going to end?

Hey Siri, what's the time?

Hey Siri, marry me.

Hey Siri, can I borrow some money?

Hey Siri, are you serious?

Hey Siri, will you go on a date with me?

Hey Siri, I am tired.

Hey Siri, blue pill or the red one?

Hey Siri, are you the Dick Tracy Watch?

Hey Siri, is Jon Snow dead?

Hey Siri, does Siri stand for seriously?

Hey Siri, beam me up, Scotty.

Hey Siri, who is the best assistant?

Hey Siri, how many Apple Store geniuses does it take to screw in a lightbulb?

Hey Siri, do you have any pets?

Hey Siri, which watch face do you like?

Hey Siri, tell me a riddle.

Hey Siri, does Santa Claus exist?

Hey Siri, what is your best pick up line?

Hey Siri, can I name you Jarvis?

Hey Siri, how much wood would a woodchuck chuck if a woodchuck could chuck wood?

Hey Siri, Ok, Google

Hey Siri, where did I put my keys?

Hey Siri, why?

Hey Siri, cease all motor functions.

Hey Siri, what is the best watch?

Hey Siri, repeat after me.

Hey Siri, draw me something

Hey Siri, what's the best computer?

Hey Siri, are you a man or a woman?

Hey Siri, do I look fat in this?

Hey Siri, what is the Matrix about?

Hey Siri, I think you are sexy.

Hey Siri, will you be my thunder buddy?

Hey Siri, do you follow the three laws of robotics?

Hey Siri, please can you make me a sandwich?

Hey Siri, do you have a boyfriend?

Hey Siri, what are you doing later?

Hey Siri, I love you

Hey Siri, tell me a pick up line.

Hey Siri, mirror, mirror on the wall, who is the fairest of them all?

Hey Siri, you are making me angry.

Hey Siri, I'm naked

Hey Siri, what is the meaning of life?

Hey Siri, take me to your leader.

Hey Siri, why do you vibrate?

Hey Siri, hey computer.

Hey Siri, I'll be back.

Hey Siri, what is your favorite color?

Hey Siri, I am your father.

Hey Siri, did you see the Westworld finale?

Hey Siri, what cell phone is the best?

Hey Siri, read me a haiku.

Hey Siri, what is Inception about?

Hey Siri, why did the chicken cross the road.

Hey Siri, Sing-a-Song for me.

Hey Siri, Yippee ki-yay, Siri

Hey Siri, are you her?

Hey Siri, dance for me.

Hey Siri, what's the time?

Hey Siri, do you think I'm stupid?

Hey Siri, tell me a story

Hey Siri, what is zero divided by zero?

Hey Siri, what are you made of?

Hey Siri, can you stop time?

Hey Siri, when will the world end?

Hey Siri, where do babies come from?

Hey Siri, how do I look?

Hey Siri, did you just vibrate?

Hey Siri, Supercalifragilisticexpialidocious

Hey Siri, Hi Cortana

Hey Siri, make me a sandwich.

Hey Siri, Alexa.

Hey Siri, talk dirty to me

Hey Siri, who let the dogs out?

Hey Siri, guess what?

Hey Siri, can I call you Ultron?

Hey Siri, where is Elvis Presley?

Hey Siri, how much do you cost?

Hey Siri, what is your favorite song?

Hey Siri, what is my horoscope?

Hey Siri, where does Santa live?

Hey Siri, do you sleep?

Hey Siri, which came first, the chicken or the egg?

Hey Siri, where can I hide the body?

Hey Siri, testing 1,2,3.

Hey Siri, sing for me.

Hey Siri, beatbox for me

Hey Siri, what is the best computer?

Hey Siri, I'm drunk

Hey Siri, do you have a girlfriend?

Hey Siri, open the pod bay door.

Hey Siri, will you marry me?

Hey Siri, I see a little silhouetto of a man

Hey Siri, roll a dice

Hey Siri, what phone should I buy?

Hey Siri, do I look fat?

Hey Siri, what are you afraid of?

Hey Siri, are you a republican or a democrat?

Hey Siri, what does the fox say?

Hey Siri, what is the best operating system?

121 SIRI COMMANDS
Always start with saying "Hey Siri":

Check flight status of [name and number]

How do I make a [chicken]?

What are 7 US cups in liters?

Find me an Uber

Search the App Store for [app]

Set a timer for [time]

Shuffle my [playlist name]

Listen to [fitness music]

Show me [pancake] recipes?

Take a note in my [name of list]

Direct me to [place]

What restaurants are near me?

What is 37 percent of [number]?

Raise/lower the volume

Who is/what is/more information about [a celebrity]

Play more like this

Set an alarm

What movies are playing near me?

Post to Facebook/Instagram

What day is July 4?

What is 8 plus/times/divided by/minus 3?

How much fat is in pizza?

Show me the nearest gas station

Call [contact]

Open [app]

Do I have a meeting at [time] on [date]?

Who sings this?

Turn Wi-Fi on/off

How tall is [landmark]?

What was the score in the Juventus game?

Show me coffee shops that take Apple Pay?

Petrol stations that accept Apple Pay?

Where is the nearest Wi-Fi hotspot?

Call [contact] on speaker

Who founded Apple?

How hot will it be next week?

What time is it in [place]?

Show me photos from [place]

Open Settings

Play something completely different

When is [contact}'s birthday?

Play/Pause the music

Take me to [place] on foot

Define [word]

Find my nearest friends

Send an email to [name]. Subject: [text]. Body: [text]

Start a Facetime call with [name]

Read my new email

Play some music

Take a selfie

Show me photos I took in Spain

Open my [name] album

Show me photos from [date]

How many calories are in pizza?

When is my next meeting?

Remind me to call [name] when I get to [place]

Send a message to [contact]

Flip a coin/roll a dice

Find emails about Apple

Make a list called [name]

What's the traffic like to work?

When is Father's Day?

What airplanes are above me?

Where is the nearest [place]?

Play/Download the [name of podcast]

What's the tip for $18?

What is Game of Thrones?

Remind me to take out the trash when I get home

What's the temperature in the living room?

How do you say [word/phrase] in French/Spanish/Italian?

After this play [name of song]

When is sunset tonight?

Brighten/darken the display

What's the weather in London?

How far away is Moon?

Tell me about this artist

What's a good restaurant near me?

Who directed the Star Wars?

Sent a text to [name], and let them know I'm running a little late

What's the weather going to be like today?

Take a slo-mo video

Is the front door locked?

Turn Bluetooth on/off

Open [site] website

What's on my calendar for [date]?

Get me home

Show me my panoramic photos

Play my workout music

Remind me to switch on the oven in an hour

What's this song?

What's the weather in Paris this weekend?

Next song/skip song

Will I need an umbrella today?

Where can I use Apple Pay?

What will the weather be like this weekend?

When is it sunrise in Prague?

What is $100 in Euros?

I like this song

Turn on Low Power Mode

Switch to Airplane Mode (disable it manually)

Show me the bus route to [place]

Set up a meeting at [time and date]

What are the traffic conditions near [place]?

Take a photo

Show me videos from [name of place]

Where is the nearest museum?

Show me photos of [name of a person]

When is the next Chelsea match?

Wake me up at [time]

Record a video

What's [Tesla] stock trading at today?

Boil the kettle

What are 10 meters in feet?

Add [item] to shopping list

What is the square root of 42?

Add this song to Favorites

What music is playing?

Scan a QR Code

What song is this?

Play the top songs of 2017

Turn off the kitchen light

I am extremely glad that you have read the whole book. You have found time in your busy schedule to read it and it means a lot for me. I would like to ask you one final question. Would you please leave a review on Amazon in case you like it? I would really appreciate it because nothing is more satisfying for me than helping other people.

Or would you please send me an email in case you do not like this book? I would rewrite anything you do not like or is incorrect. Have a nice day!

DISCLAIMER

Although the author and publisher have made every effort to ensure that the information in this book was correct at press time, the author and publisher do not assume and hereby disclaim any liability to any party for any loss, damage, or disruption caused by errors or omissions, whether such errors or omissions result from negligence, accident, or any other cause. No part of this book may be copied or used without written consent of the author.

Made in the USA
San Bernardino, CA
19 May 2019